Original title:
Shades of Me

Copyright © 2024 Creative Arts Management OÜ
All rights reserved.

Author: Liam Sterling
ISBN HARDBACK: 978-9916-88-930-5
ISBN PAPERBACK: 978-9916-88-931-2

The Allure of Contradiction.

In silence, screams reside,
A dance of shadows, side by side.
Sweetness found in bitter pain,
Nature's joy is wrapped in rain.

Flames that warm, yet also burn,
In every loss, we still discern.
Hope and despair, hand in hand,
Life's great puzzle, unplanned yet grand.

Reflections in a Kaleidoscope.

Glimmers of light spin and play,
Fragments of dreams dance in dismay.
Colors shifting in endless forms,
Truth found in chaotic norms.

Each turn reveals a different view,
A blend of old pierces through new.
Nature and art in bright display,
Whispers of thoughts that drift away.

Colors of My Silent Testimony.

Shades of blue, my heart in pain,
Greens of hope in fields of grain.
Yellows gleam of joy's refrain,
Reds of passion, love's domain.

Every hue tells a tale inside,
In every corner, dreams reside.
A palette rich, yet deeply shy,
Tunes of silence, they never lie.

The Spectrum of Self.

I wear my colors, bright and bold,
Layers of stories yet untold.
In shades of doubt and strokes of grace,
Each moment finds its rightful place.

A prism fractured, light defined,
Fragments of thought, intertwined.
In echoes soft, my voice does swell,
This canvas painted, who can tell?

The Palette of Existence

Colors dance on canvas wide,
Life's hues blend with every stride.
Whispers of joy, strokes of pain,
Each moment crafted, none in vain.

Shades of laughter, tints of tears,
Mirrors of hopes, reflections of fears.
Every brushstroke tells a tale,
In this masterpiece, we prevail.

Dreams like colors, vivid and bright,
Painting the day, embracing the night.
In the chaos, beauty grows,
The palette of life, forever glows.

Echoes in My Silence

In the quiet, echoes sound,
Whispers of thoughts that circle round.
A world unseen but deeply felt,
In silence, the heart can melt.

Every pause, a voice within,
Solitude's song, a gentle spin.
Moments linger, shadows play,
In the hush, my dreams can sway.

Chasing echoes, softly clear,
In my silence, I draw near.
With every heartbeat, I define,
The melody of this life of mine.

Tints of Experience

Every experience, a brush in hand,
Colors blend as I take a stand.
From shadows cast to brightness found,
In every moment, layers abound.

Textures rich, with stories weave,
In the fabric of life, I believe.
Each tinge a lesson, a memory bright,
Guiding my path with gentle light.

Past and present, interlace,
In each layer, I find my place.
With tints of laughter, shades of strife,
I paint the canvas of my life.

Layers of Identity

Beneath the surface, layers lie,
Each one tells of who am I.
Peeling back, I find my core,
A tapestry of evermore.

Rooted deep in dreams and fears,
Hopes entwined with passing years.
In each layer, lessons reside,
A journey vast, I cannot hide.

Faces worn like masks we wear,
In every glance, a story there.
Discovering depth, I celebrate,
The layers of love that shape my fate.

A Canvas of Life's Contrasts

Bright hues clash with muted shades,
A dance of light in twilight fades.
Joy bursts forth, shadows intertwine,
Life's tapestry, both coarse and fine.

Colors bleed, the edges fray,
Moments lost, yet here they stay.
Every brushstroke tells a tale,
In vibrant whispers, hearts unveil.

The Palette of Woven Memories

Threads of gold and softest pink,
In every hue, we stop and think.
Each woven strand, a moment caught,
In fabric's grace, our battles fought.

Faded colors, stories worn,
In quiet rooms, dreams are borne.
Each touch recalls a face, a place,
In woven hearts, we find our grace.

Layers of Laughter and Sorrow

Laughter lingers like a sweet refrain,
Yet underneath, a trace of pain.
Layers stack, both light and dark,
In every moment, there's a spark.

Joy cascades, then ebbs away,
Yet hope remains, come what may.
Tears mix with laughter's wild song,
In life's embrace, we all belong.

Collage of Inner Whispers

Fragments of dreams in scattered light,
Voices murmur in the quiet night.
Thoughts collide, a vibrant fray,
In whispered truths, we find our way.

Images dance in shadows deep,
Silent promises, secrets to keep.
In this collage of heart and mind,
A world of wonder we seek to find.

The Layers of My Heart's Painting

Each stroke a shade of silent fear,
Blending love with hues of regret.
The canvas soft beneath my tear,
A masterpiece that's not quite set.

Time adds more depth, a whisper's touch,
Colors clash and yet align.
In chaos found, I cherish such,
Each layer tells my heart's design.

Tones that Speak of My Journey

Footprints mark the roads I've tried,
Brushed in tones of pale and bold.
Through valleys deep and mountains wide,
My spirit weaves its tale of old.

With each step, a note is played,
Resonating through my core.
The echoes of the choices made,
Create the symphony I adore.

The Portrait of Contradiction

Light and shadow dance entwined,
A visage forged with truths and lies.
What's spoken and what's confined,
Form the depths beneath my skies.

In every glance, a story swells,
Of love and loss, of joy and pain.
With every brush, a secret tells,
The beauty found in every stain.

The Eloquent Colors of Vulnerability

Soft pastels of whispered fears,
Bold primaries of open heart.
Each color speaks through silent tears,
Revealing where my truths depart.

Through gentle strokes, I share my tale,
In bravery, I let it show.
Beneath the surface, raw and frail,
The art of being is to grow.

A Journey through Invisible Hues

In silence, colors blend and fade,
Whispers of shades in the twilight made.
A road untraveled, a dream untold,
Where hues emerge, both brave and bold.

With every step, the spectrum shifts,
Emotions dance, like drifting gifts.
A canvas stretched beyond our sight,
In every shadow, there glows a light.

The Chorus of Inner Colors

A melody plays within my heart,
Each note a hue, a vibrant part.
Some sweet like sunsets, some dark like night,
Together they sing, a symphony bright.

With brushes of laughter, strokes of fear,
They paint my thoughts, so crystal clear.
In this chorus, we find our voice,
In silent stories, we rejoice.

The Unseen Brush of Emotion

In depths unknown, I feel the sway,
A brush unseen, it guides my way.
Each flick and stroke, a feeling new,
In artful chaos, the heart breaks through.

Tears of joy, and shadows cast,
A palette rich, memories amassed.
Through gentle whispers, colors flow,
Emotions linger, steady and slow.

The Canvas Beneath My Skin

Layers hidden, where stories lie,
Beneath the surface, dreams can fly.
Each scar a shade, each laugh a stroke,
A masterpiece born from all we spoke.

As life unfolds, the canvas changes,
With every heartbeat, the art rearranges.
In every moment, I find my truth,
The canvas breathes, alive with youth.

Fragments of Identity

In a mirror, shards collide,
Whispers of who we choose to hide.
Layers peel like paint from walls,
Echoes rise as a silence calls.

Stories stitched with threads of care,
A quilt of lives, an unseen share.
Each piece a glimpse of what we feel,
In fragments, truth begins to heal.

Reflections spark our hidden dreams,
In broken bits, the past redeems.
Unraveled tales in tangled thoughts,
In every flaw, a lesson taught.

A Tapestry of Unseen Voices

Gentle whispers weave the night,
Colors blend in pure delight.
Threads of hope and threads of pain,
Silent songs, a sweet refrain.

In the weave, a tale unfolds,
Stories rich, like strands of gold.
Unseen voices in the dark,
Each a heart, each a spark.

Patterns form in silent grace,
A canvas of each human face.
Together we create a scene,
A tapestry of what has been.

Shimmering Facets of Existence

Diamonds dance in twilight's glow,
Every facet tells us so.
Life's reflections, bright and dim,
A spectrum vast, we swim within.

Moments twinkle, lost or found,
In the silence, joy resounds.
Shadows whisper truths profound,
In each heartbeat, love unbound.

A kaleidoscope of chance and fate,
Infinite paths that resonate.
Embrace the shimmer, let it flow,
For in this light, our spirits grow.

Portraits of an Evolving Soul

Brushstrokes linger on the page,
Capturing life at every stage.
With every line, a tale is spun,
Portraits of battles lost and won.

In soft hues, the heart reveals,
Struggles faced, and hope that heals.
What once was dark begins to light,
In every shadow, a spark ignites.

Layers deepen as we strive,
Our essence blooms, we come alive.
An evolving soul, rich and bold,
In every portrait, stories told.

The Dance of Radiant Dualities

In shadows and in light, we twirl,
Two spirits bound, a cosmic swirl.
One step forward, one step back,
Harmony sings in each heartbeat's track.

The night embraces the dawn's first kiss,
In this balance, there's sacred bliss.
A playful tug like the ebbing tide,
In the radiant dance, we both reside.

Reflections shimmer on the surface clear,
In the duality, we persevere.
With whispered thoughts, both soft and loud,
We find our place within the crowd.

Each turn and twist, a graceful sway,
Revealing truths we often dismay.
In this dance, we boldly tread,
A glorious blend of feelings spread.

Introspection in Vibrant Colors

Upon the canvas of my mind,
Each hue reveals what's intertwined.
With strokes of red for fiery dreams,
And hues of blue, with silent schemes.

Amidst the green, where hope resides,
In vivid splashes, my heart confides.
Yellows bright spark joy anew,
As shadows dance in shades of blue.

A palette rich, emotions flow,
In vibrant tones, my spirit grows.
Through every layer, I lay bare,
The colors of my soul declare.

Each mixing shade tells stories deep,
Of secrets kept and dreams to reap.
With introspection, I find my way,
In these vivid hues, I choose to stay.

The Quiet Palette of Existence

In soft pastels of dawn's embrace,
A muted world, a tranquil space.
The whispers of the morning light,
Awakening dreams that drift from night.

Colors blend in gentle sighs,
In quiet moments, the spirit flies.
Each shade subdued, yet filled with grace,
In this palette, we find our place.

The gray of clouds, the brown of earth,
Reflecting all of nature's worth.
In silence speaks the heart's own song,
In this calm, we find where we belong.

With each stroke of time's own hand,
Life's quiet whispers gently stand.
A canvas bare, yet full of life,
The palette shows both peace and strife.

Shimmering Threads of My Narrative

Woven tales in gleaming thread,
Stories linger where footsteps tread.
Each fiber glows with vibrant hue,
Tales of joy, and sorrows too.

In tapestry of days gone by,
Moments captured, hearts will sigh.
With shimmering strands, my life unfolds,
Adventures brave, and dreams retold.

The needle pierces through the night,
Stitching love with all its might.
Each knot a memory tightly bound,
In vibrant threads, my truth is found.

Through tales of laughter, threads do weave,
In intricate patterns, I believe.
Shimmering paths converge and part,
Crafting the narrative of my heart.

The Grayscale of My Experience

In shadows where memories dwell,
Life's moments begin to swell.
Each hue a story left behind,
A canvas dull, yet well-defined.

Through time's lens, I walk with grace,
In grayscale, I find my place.
The whispers of the past unfold,
In muted tones, my heart is bold.

The monochrome of days gone by,
Reflects the laughter, love, and sigh.
Every shade, a lesson learned,
In silence, life's fire burned.

Yet in this world devoid of flair,
I seek the light, the vibrant air.
With each step, I shift the tone,
From shades of gray, I find my own.

Palette of Past and Present

Brushstrokes blend in vivid grace,
The past and now in warm embrace.
Each color speaks of times gone by,
A vibrant tale beneath the sky.

Memories float like shades of blue,
Of love and loss, both tried and true.
The swirls of green hold hope anew,
While golden light brings visions through.

With every hue, a story blends,
A canvas where the heart transcends.
Rich reds of passion, deep and bright,
Unfolding dreams in the soft twilight.

Together they form a life well-lived,
A palette mixed, a gift to give.
In each brushstroke, joy unspun,
The past and present, forever one.

The Hidden Vibrance

In corners tucked, where shadows sway,
Lies vibrant life, in soft decay.
A spectrum waits for eyes to see,
The thrill of what will always be.

Among the cracks, the colors peek,
With whispers bright, they softly speak.
In silence, sparks of joy ignite,
A burst of life, a soft delight.

The hidden shades of every day,
In forgotten nooks, they gently play.
Each brush of light, a secret shared,
In quiet spaces, love is bared.

Unlock the door to what's unseen,
Find beauty where it has not been.
In every heart, a vibrant call,
The hidden hues that bind us all.

Echoing Tints of Truth

Reflections flash in colors clear,
The truth exposed, both far and near.
Each tint a tale that time unfolds,
A history wrapped in vibrant folds.

With every stroke, emotions blend,
In shades of love that never end.
The echoes rise, a song divine,
In hues of honesty, we shine.

From deep maroon to bright sky blue,
The palette breathes, the heart stays true.
In every whisper, colors dance,
A heartfelt truth, a perfect chance.

As layers peel, so do the lies,
Beneath the surface, clarity lies.
Echoing tints reveal the core,
In vibrant truth, we're evermore.

Contrasts in the Mirror

In twilight's glow, shadows creep,
A world unseen, secrets deep.
Light whispers truths, dark holds the past,
In the mirror's gaze, moments cast.

Laughter echoes where silence dwells,
Joy and sorrow weave their spells.
Colors clash, yet blend so fine,
Contrasts linger, yours and mine.

Reflections pulse in a rhythmic dance,
Chasing dreams and lost romance.
Each flicker tells a story grand,
Of the life we build, hand in hand.

In perfect chaos, we find clarity,
A bond forged through duality.
With every glance, we redefine,
The art of living, yours and mine.

Radiant Reflections

Sunlight spills on morning dew,
A golden hue in skies so blue.
Each drop a mirror, bright and clear,
Capturing dreams that linger near.

Beneath the shade, shadows play,
Silent thoughts drift softly away.
Whispers of hope in the gentle light,
Radiance blooms, banishing night.

Colors collide, a vibrant scene,
Nature's palette, pure and keen.
In every heartbeat, the world conspires,
To paint our lives with love's desires.

In stillness found, reflections rise,
Holding the depth of endless skies.
In every glance, the beauty we see,
Radiates softly, you and me.

The Dance of Duality

Two sides of a coin, spinning fast,
Moments fleeting, shadows cast.
In harmony, they twist and twirl,
A dance of light in a world unfurled.

Passion ignites, tempered with grace,
A fiery heart in a calm embrace.
The night whispers truths, the day sings light,
In every clash, magic ignites.

Boundless journeys through space and time,
Each step forward, a silent rhyme.
In duality's arms, we find our way,
Navigating the night and day.

Together we move, a swirling flight,
Illuminated by the fabric of night.
In the dance of life, we seek and find,
The balance of hearts, forever entwined.

Shadows and Luminescence

In shadowed corners, secrets lie,
Softly spoken, a silent sigh.
With every flicker, a spark ignites,
Illuminating the darkest nights.

Beneath the glow of stars above,
Shadows whisper tales of love.
In twilight's grasp, dreams take flight,
Chasing the echoes of fading light.

Contrast plays in the night's embrace,
Transforming fears into grace.
Each glimmering moment, a chance to see,
The beauty in what is meant to be.

In shadows cast by the dawn's first gleam,
Luminescence fuels the waking dream.
In every heartbeat, the world aligns,
A dance of light where our soul shines.

The Colors I Wear

In shades of blue, I find my peace,
A tranquil hue that lacks no lease.
With fiery red, my passions flare,
Each color tells a tale I share.

A whisper of green in my soul does bloom,
Nature's embrace, dispelling gloom.
Golden yellow shines with joy,
Each tone a thread, no dark can destroy.

Through purples deep, I seek the night,
Mysteries wrapped in velvet light.
The colors mingle, dance, and sway,
A canvas bright, my heart's array.

Manifestations of My Spirit

I rise like mist at dawn's slight break,
An echo soft, no heart to shake.
With strength like roots that grip the ground,
In silence, sacred truths are found.

Waves crash fiercely, yet calm I stand,
Emotions whirl, like grains of sand.
A flicker bright, a blazing star,
In stillness, know just who you are.

Each breath I take, a whispered prayer,
In the vast universe, I declare.
All fragments of the soul's vast lore,
I am the spirit, forevermore.

Threads of Intricacy

Each thread a story, woven tight,
In patterns bold, they catch the light.
A tapestry of moments spun,
In every curve, a battle won.

Fingers dance, the loom does hum,
Creating beauty, beating drums.
In vibrant hues of dream and dread,
My history stitched, my future spread.

Through tangled knots, I find my way,
In woven strands, I choose to stay.
Delicate ties, yet strong and grand,
The threads of life, in my own hand.

The Symphony of Self

In melodies sweet, my heart does play,
   A symphony that guides my way.
   Notes of laughter, chords of pain,
   Each sound a star in life's refrain.

In rhythms bold, my pulse does beat,
   A harmony where shadows meet.
   With whispers soft, and echoes loud,
   I dance alive, no fear, no shroud.

The cadence rises, and then it falls,
   Each note a truth, in silence calls.
   A timeless score, my spirit's guide,
   In every note, the world inside.

The Tapestry Within

Threads of color weave and twine,
Stories hidden, designs divine.
In every stitch, a secret glows,
A tapestry of life, it flows.

Whispers of dreams in the fabric speak,
Soft and gentle, they rise and peak.
Each moment captured, a fleeting breath,
Woven memories, defying death.

Patterns shifting, a dance of grace,
Time unraveled in this sacred space.
Boundless beauty, from joy to strife,
A reflection of the tapestry of life.

In the depths, a story to find,
A masterpiece birthed from the heart and mind.
Through storms and silence, the threads remain,
A vibrant weave, a joyful refrain.

Whispers of My Essence

In shadows cast by fading light,
I find the whispers, soft and slight.
Echoes of thoughts from deep within,
The essence of my soul's true skin.

Like autumn leaves, the colors spin,
A dance of whispers that pull me in.
Beneath the surface, currents flow,
Secrets hidden, treasures glow.

Each breath a sigh, each sigh a plea,
Unraveling the depths of me.
In tranquil moments, I hear the tone,
The whispers telling I'm not alone.

With open heart and willing ear,
I embrace these whispers, holding dear.
They guide me gently through night and day,
Unveiling truths along the way.

Fragments of My Soul

Scattered pieces, lost yet found,
Shattered mirrors make a sound.
Reflecting shadows, light unveils,
Fragments dance in whispered tales.

In every shard, a story lies,
The laughter, the tears, the soft goodbyes.
Held together by threads of grace,
A mosaic forms in this sacred space.

Searching deep within the cracks,
Rediscovering the heart's own tracks.
Every fragment holds its place,
Creating beauty in the embrace.

Though brokenness paints a weary mark,
Each piece becomes a vital spark.
United now, they sing and roam,
Fragments of my soul, a vibrant home.

Variations of Being

In every breath, a new refrain,
Shifting tides, a dance of gain.
Moments woven, bits of grace,
Variations of life in this space.

From dawn to dusk, a world unfolds,
Each chapter penned with dreams untold.
Colors blend and shapes combine,
In the rhythm of life, we intertwine.

From laughter bright to whispers soft,
In highs and lows, our spirits aloft.
Every variation tells a tale,
A wondrous journey, we set sail.

Embracing change, we learn to see,
The beauty of our vast complexity.
In every heartbeat, every sigh,
Variations of being, we learn to fly.

Celestial Patterns

Stars above in silent dance,
Whispers of a cosmic chance.
Galaxies weave a tale untold,
In the night, their beauty bold.

Moonlight drapes a silver veil,
Guiding dreams on night's frail sail.
Comets trace their fiery paths,
In the dark, igniting laughs.

Constellations form a guide,
Mapping hearts where hopes abide.
In every twinkle, secrets lie,
An astral song, a lullaby.

Awash in wonder, we behold,
Through the heavens, stories unfold.
With each gaze upward, we connect,
Celestial patterns, hearts reflect.

Nuances and Nurture

In whispered tones, the world awakes,
Subtle shifts, the heart remakes.
Soft hues of dawn, a tender start,
Nature's brush paints every heart.

In every leaf, a tale to tell,
Of storms weathered, of sunlit dwell.
The rustling breeze, a gentle guide,
Inviting peace where shadows hide.

Colors mingle in embrace,
Each moment holds a fleeting grace.
With every breath, we cultivate,
The beauty found in love's estate.

So let us cherish every hue,
In nuances, our spirits renew.
With nurture born from simple things,
Life's soft song, a symphony sings.

The Unfolding Canvas

Blank and vast, the canvas lies,
Whispers of potential rise.
Brushes poised, with colors bright,
Dreams take flight in swirling light.

Every stroke, a story shared,
In hues of hope, our hearts declared.
Layers built with love and pain,
Art of life, our truths contain.

In this space, we dare to play,
Creating worlds in bold array.
With every color, shadows blend,
An endless journey that transcends.

From empty slate to vibrant scene,
Each new vision blooms between.
The unfolding canvas of our fate,
Awaits our touch, it's never late.

Journey Through My Layers

Beneath the surface, stories sleep,
In winding paths, secrets keep.
Each layer whispers of the past,
A journey deep, a truth amassed.

With fragile threads, I weave my tale,
In every fold, the winds prevail.
Roots run deep, yet branches sway,
In harmony, they find their way.

Each layer speaks of love and fear,
Of battles fought and dreams held dear.
Through shifting sands, I carve my name,
In every challenge, find the flame.

So join me in this quest for light,
Through layers vast, we'll take our flight.
In the depths of me, you'll surely find,
A tapestry of heart and mind.

A Journey through My Colorful Echoes

In whispers soft, the colors blend,
They dance like shadows, round the bend.
Each hue a tale, a sweet refrain,
A symphony of joy and pain.

Through streets of gold and skies of blue,
I wander wide, I wander true.
With every step, the echoes rise,
Painting whispers 'neath the skies.

The crimson blush of morn's first kiss,
A touch of grace, a fleeting bliss.
Emerald fields, where dreams unfold,
In vibrant realms, my heart behold.

At twilight's call, the colors fade,
A tapestry of night, well laid.
In silence now, my spirit flies,
Through echoes bright, beneath the skies.

Reflective Tides of the Heart

Upon the shore, the waves do sigh,
They whisper secrets, low and high.
With every crest, a heart laid bare,
A mirror held, the soul laid fair.

The tides that rise, they bring and take,
A gentle pull, a soft heartache.
With silver moons, the waters gleam,
Reflecting all, a wistful dream.

In moments fraught with joy and pain,
The ocean's breath does speak my name.
A dance of tides, a sacred art,
The ebb and flow of every heart.

So let me drift on this wide sea,
A journey deep, just waves and me.
In every swell, a lesson learned,
In heart's embrace, my spirit burned.

The Chromatic Realm of Dreams

In dreams I walk through colors bright,
A kaleidoscope of pure delight.
With every step, the shades unfold,
A tapestry of stories told.

Golden fields with sapphire skies,
A world where imagination flies.
The lilac mist at dusk's embrace,
Invites the night, a velvet space.

Through burgundy and emerald lanes,
I lose myself in music's strains.
Where every corner sparks a tale,
In chromatic bliss, I set my sail.

With dreams to guide, and stars to chase,
I wander free, a timeless grace.
In realms of hues, I find my peace,
In colors bright, my soul's release.

Echoes of My Inner Canvas

Colors swirl in silent grace,
Memories of time and space.
Shadows dance, they come alive,
In this world where echoes thrive.

Brushstrokes of a restless mind,
In every corner, secrets bind.
Voices linger, softly sigh,
Underneath the painted sky.

Dreams take flight, like birds in spring,
Each hue a story, joy they bring.
Layers whisper, deep and wide,
In this canvas, feelings hide.

Fragile notes on twilight's breath,
Artistry entwined with death.
Life and loss, they intertwine,
In the echoes, I define.

Tones of a Hidden Heart

Deep within, the colors blend,
Softening shadows, they extend.
Whispers wrapped in velvet night,
Tones emerge, embracing light.

Every heartbeat, rhythm's glow,
In the silence, secrets flow.
Hidden layers start to show,
As the gentle breezes blow.

Songs of silence, softly played,
In this heart, no colors fade.
Harmonies of love remain,
In the depths, where truth sustains.

Unveiling dreams with tender grace,
Each tone reveals a sacred space.
In the quiet, let it start,
Echoes found in hidden heart.

Whispers in Varied Hues

Brush the air with gentle sighs,
In the twilight, color flies.
Softly whispered, colors blend,
In the stillness, they descend.

Crimson dreams and azure skies,
Palette shifts as daylight dies.
Hues entwined in tender glow,
In this realm, the secrets flow.

Echoed laughter, shadows dance,
In every hue, a second chance.
Whispers weave through summer's days,
In their path, my spirit sways.

Layers rich and deeply spun,
Every whisper tells of fun.
In the canvas, life renews,
With the whispers in varied hues.

The Palette of My Being

Mixing colors on the brink,
In every shade, I find my link.
Vibrant strokes of love and fear,
The palette holds what I hold dear.

Crimson rage and sapphire peace,
Blend together, never cease.
Every hue, a part of me,
In this art, I feel so free.

Canvas stretched with hopes and dreams,
Life's mosaic, bursting seams.
Textures face the light of day,
In the palette, I will stay.

With each brush, the truth revealed,
In these colors, I am healed.
Painting life with every breath,
In this palette lies no death.

Spectrum of Hidden Chronicles

In shadows where the whispers blend,
Lies a tale that silently bends.
Colors flicker in the night,
Telling stories out of sight.

A canvas painted with time's grace,
Every hue in a sacred space.
Memories dance in soft light's glow,
Secrets that only dreams can know.

Each stroke tells of love and pain,
Wisps of joy, echoes of rain.
Fragments captured, never still,
Life unfolds with a painter's will.

Within the realm where colors blend,
Chronicles rise and softly transcend.
A spectrum vivid, quietly sought,
In each heart, a story caught.

Hues of a Traveling Heart

Wanderlust stirs the quiet soul,
Chasing sunsets, feeling whole.
Each path leads to colors bright,
In fleeting moments wrapped in light.

Soft echoes of distant lands,
Where love blooms and time expands.
With every step, new colors rise,
Painting dreams beneath the skies.

Violet mountains, sapphire seas,
Every journey whispers, 'please'.
Hues of kindness, shades of grace,
A traveling heart finds its place.

Embracing all that life imparts,
With every mile, it beats and charts.
An odyssey of vibrant days,
Crafting love in endless ways.

The Tapestry of Unraveled Moments

Threads of time woven so fine,
In every moment, lives entwine.
Patterns rich with laughter's sound,
In silence, deeper truths are found.

Stitches formed with joy and tears,
Echoes resonating through years.
Each memory, a vibrant thread,
A tapestry where dreams are spread.

Colors shift with every breath,
Life's masterpiece, a dance with death.
Unraveled moments delicately spun,
In the twilight, where life's begun.

A quilt of love, sorrow, and grace,
In every heart, a sacred space.
As stories weave and time consumes,
We find our strength in the vibrant rooms.

Echoes in Vivid Tints

Whispers echo in vivid tints,
Where every note and color glints.
A symphony of hearts unchained,
In vibrant hues, the soul is stained.

Laughter mingles with shadows cast,
Threads of present, ties to past.
Moments dance in splendid light,
Painting dreams in endless flight.

Raindrops melody, sunbeam rays,
Harmony in nature's plays.
With every pulse, the colors speak,
Showing truths that seem unique.

Echoes linger, soft and clear,
In every shade, the world draws near.
A canvas brushed with love's intent,
In vivid tints, our lives are spent.

Portrait of a Woven Soul

In threads of gold, a story spins,
Silent whispers, where it begins.
With every stitch, a memory known,
A tapestry rich, the heart has grown.

Colors blend, they dance in light,
Faded shadows, a glimpse of night.
In every fold, a tale to tell,
Woven tight, where secrets dwell.

From fibers strong, the fabric breathes,
In quiet moments, it weaves and weaves.
A portrait framed in joy and pain,
A woven soul, forever reigns.

Light and Dark in Equal Measure

In the dawn's glow, shadows play,
Harmony found in night's ballet.
With each heartbeat, both sides reflect,
A dance of light, a tone direct.

Stars emerge, embrace the void,
In silence made, the dark's enjoyed.
Flashes bright, where hope ignites,
In stillness, find the brightest sights.

Together they rise, an endless fight,
Breath of day, breath of night.
In every soul, this dual trace,
Light and dark share a sacred space.

The Undercurrents of Essence

Beneath the surface, currents flow,
Silent whispers, an undertow.
Glimmers of truth in depths concealed,
An essence strong, yet unrevealed.

Waves of feeling crash and sway,
A hidden light in shadows play.
Each emotion, a drop in time,
In the still waters, the heart's rhyme.

Ripples dance, stories unfold,
In silence vast, the brave and bold.
A mirrored depth, reflections gleam,
The undercurrents weave a dream.

A Spectrum of Unexpressed Feelings

In muted tones, the heart's refrain,
A palette rich, yet bound in chain.
Each hue a thought, a silent scream,
A spectrum wide, a hidden dream.

Colors clash in quiet wars,
Where hope blooms bright behind closed doors.
In every shade, a story waits,
Unexpressed love, that still berates.

From joy to sorrow, shades unfold,
In silence fine, emotions hold.
A vibrant mesh, the soul's design,
A spectrum vast, forever mine.

The Prism of My Life

Light breaks through the glass,
Creating colors bright and fast.
Shadows dance with every hue,
Reflecting dreams that feel so true.

Moments flicker in the sun,
Each shade tells of battles won.
Rainbows arch, they lead the way,
To the dawn of a new day.

Fragments of joy interlace,
In this endless, vibrant space.
Every tint, a memory drawn,
In the prism, I am reborn.

Through the spectrum, I shall glide,
With every color, I confide.
In the brilliance, I find peace,
In my prism, dreams increase.

Layers of Forgotten Dreams

Beneath the dust, they linger still,
Whispers of hope that time can't kill.
Veiled in layers, stories sleep,
In quiet corners, secrets creep.

Each fold hides a memory dear,
Faded laughter, silent tear.
Unraveled threads, they weave my path,
Imagined futures, lost in wrath.

Cracked foundations, yet they stand,
A tapestry, by fate's own hand.
Through the chaos, beauty blooms,
In forgotten dreams, hope resumes.

With gentle hands, I peel away,
The weight of night, the light of day.
Each layer reveals a part of me,
In the ruins, I learn to be.

Mosaic of Unclaimed Stories

Shattered pieces, bright and bold,
Fragments waiting to be told.
Each tile holds a silent plea,
In the mosaic, I find me.

Color spills from heart's embrace,
Stories etched on every face.
In the chaos, I make sense,
Unclaimed stories, past defense.

Cascading echoes fill the air,
Fleeting time, yet always there.
In the glass, reflections play,
Whispers beckon, lead the way.

With every stitch, my heart aligns,
In this mosaic, life combines.
A work of art, both flawed and fine,
In unclaimed tales, I brightly shine.

Colors that Whisper My Name

In hues that dance upon the breeze,
Soft tones that put my heart at ease.
Each shade a whisper, soft and clear,
Echoes of love that draw me near.

Crimson blush for passion's fire,
Emerald dreams that never tire.
Sapphire skies where hope takes flight,
In every color, pure delight.

Golden rays that kiss the dawn,
Cobalt seas where I belong.
Pastel shades of twilight's grace,
In vivid colors, I find my place.

With every stroke, my spirit sings,
In bursts of color, freedom brings.
These whispers call, and I respond,
In colors bold, of which I'm fond.

Reflections in a Kaleidoscope

Fragments of light dance and play,
Shifting shapes in vibrant display.
Mirrored dreams twist round and round,
In this world of wonder, I am found.

Colors blend in a fleeting glance,
Each hue sings a unique dance.
Patterns merge, then fade away,
In my heart, they'll forever stay.

Shattered pieces form a whole,
Each reflection revealing a soul.
Chaos blooms into a scene,
A patchwork of what has been.

Within this glass, I see my fears,
Yet also joy that fills with years.
In every turn, a lesson learned,
In every twist, my spirit churned.

Colors Beneath My Skin

Beneath the surface, shades reside,
Hidden hues I cannot hide.
Crimson threads of love and pain,
Whispers of joy, a vibrant rain.

Emerald whispers of hope untold,
Stories of strength buried bold.
Each scar a tale, each mark a sign,
A spectrum woven, solely mine.

Golden glimmers of laughter bright,
Dancing softly in the night.
The palette shifts with every breath,
Life's masterpiece, defying death.

In every pulse, there's a reveal,
Colors that scream, others conceal.
With every heartbeat, I embrace,
The shades of life, my truest grace.

The Spectrum of Self

A rainbow arc within my chest,
Each shade a truth, a silent quest.
In every tone, a story rings,
The essence of all that living brings.

When shadows fall, the colors rise,
In darkness, light begins to fly.
Through storms, the palette finds its way,
In every trial, I choose to stay.

Pastels of youth, bold strokes of age,
In the gallery of life, I turn the page.
Each layer thickens, each brush a choice,
In strokes of silence, I find my voice.

Lost in hues, I seek the blend,
To find myself, to start, to mend.
In every layer, I am whole,
A masterpiece, my hidden soul.

Hues of My Heart

In the quiet, colors stir,
Painting feelings, an inner blur.
Deep blues of love, rich reds of strife,
A canvas shaped by the art of life.

Soft violets whisper sweet embrace,
While yellows shine, bringing grace.
In every shade, a memory lies,
Reflecting laughter, echoing sighs.

Greys may linger, shadows cast,
Yet brighter tones speak of the past.
A symphony crafted by time's deft hand,
In hues, a vision, beautifully planned.

With every heartbeat, colors weave,
Forming the fabric of what I believe.
In each deep hue, a tender start,
I find the vibrant hues of my heart.

The Dance of My Many Masks

In the mirror, faces play,
Each a tale, night and day.
Whispers hide behind the guise,
Secrets swirl in joyful lies.

Masked in laughter, masked in tears,
Each a dance that churns my fears.
One steps lightly, one stands tall,
In this waltz, I risk it all.

Colors change with every turn,
Flickering lights in hearts that yearn.
I spin and twirl, unseen yet seen,
In this carnival, I glean.

With every mask, a lesson learned,
Through joy and pain, my spirit burned.
Yet in the dance, I feel alive,
In shadows deep, my souls survive.

Notes in a Colorful Symphony

In twilight's hush, the colors blend,
Each note a brushstroke, time to spend.
Strings and winds, a vibrant call,
Harmony that binds us all.

Through the canvas, melodies flow,
Bursting colors, rich and slow.
A saxophone's sweet, sultry cry,
Like painted skies that never die.

Amidst the chaos, rhythms pulse,
Each heartbeat syncs, life's great convulse.
Echoes dance in the cool night air,
As if the stars themselves would dare.

In every note, a story found,
Crimson dreams and whispers sound.
Together we weave, just let them soar,
A colorful symphony forevermore.

Shadows of Unspoken Thoughts

In the corner, shadows creep,
Laden secrets softly weep.
Words unspoken drift away,
In silence, they choose to stay.

Thoughts like whispers in the night,
Flicker dimly, shunning light.
A tapestry of fears and dreams,
Frayed edges whisper silent screams.

Among the gloom, my visions hide,
Buried truths that I confide.
Each shadow tells a tale untold,
In quiet corners, the heart unfolds.

Yet in this darkness, moments shine,
Ephemeral, and so divine.
For even shadows seek the sun,
In the stillness, I become one.

Refractions of an Untamed Spirit

In wild winds, my soul takes flight,
Dancing freely, day and night.
A prism's burst, my essence gleams,
Reflecting passion, rawest dreams.

Through tangled paths, I roam unchained,
In the chaos, purpose gained.
Unearthed truths beneath the skin,
A tempest's heart, fierce and thin.

Colors clash beneath the storm,
Breaking boundaries, life reborn.
Fragmented light, a brilliant show,
In every shadow, I still glow.

With courage woven through the pain,
I rise again, a phoenix slain.
Refractions bold, my spirit's spark,
In a world vibrant, I leave my mark.

Ink of Many Stories

In the quiet of the night,
Whispers float like dreams.
Each word a gentle thread,
Woven into life's seams.

Pages turn with soft intent,
Ink bleeds history's hue.
Tales of love, loss, and time,
A world painted anew.

Characters dance and leap,
Through realms of thought and fear.
With each stroke, lives unfurl,
And truths begin to clear.

So dip your quill in fate,
Let the stories unfold.
In the ink of many tales,
Lives a heart that is bold.

The Wild Brushstrokes of Destiny

Colors clash in a vibrant fight,
Fate's canvas without bounds.
Each stroke a twist of fate,
In chaos, beauty sounds.

Swirls and curves of a life unknown,
Brushes dance to a wild beat.
Paintings whisper secrets old,
As the future takes its seat.

Every splatter tells a tale,
Of choices made and lost.
In wild brushstrokes we discover,
The price of every cost.

So let the colors run amok,
Embrace the stormy skies.
In the wild brushstrokes of life,
Destiny boldly lies.

Reflections of My Many Tints

In the mirror, hues collide,
Shades of joy and pain.
Each tint reflects a story,
Caught in life's refrain.

Rust and gold, soft pastels,
Colors intertwine.
From the depths of my spirit,
To the surface, they align.

Every tint a memory,
A moment held in time.
Reflections dance with meaning,
And echo like a rhyme.

Through the spectrum of my heart,
I find a way to shine.
In reflections of my many tints,
A canvas so divine.

The Harmonious Chaos of Being

Life's melody swells and bends,
Notes collide but create.
In the chaos, harmony lies,
An ever-turning fate.

Rumbles of laughter and tears,
Each pulse a beat of heart.
In disorder, sweet rhythms bloom,
Each moment a work of art.

Every misstep a chance to grow,
Finding peace in the storm.
In the whirlwind, I discover,
The beauty to be reborn.

So embrace the complex dance,
Let the music guide the way.
In the harmonious chaos of being,
We blossom with each sway.

Portraits of the Unseen

Silent shadows drift and weave,
In corners where secrets breathe.
Whispers of lives untold,
Capturing moments, quiet and bold.

Fragments of faces lost in time,
Echoes of laughter, a distant chime.
Each glance a story, hidden away,
In the portraits that dreams convey.

Hues of sorrow, strokes of delight,
Canvas painted by day and night.
Lost in the depths of the heart,
Each unseen soul, a work of art.

In twilight's embrace, they softly call,
The unseen tales that bind us all.
A gallery rich with hopes concealed,
In these portraits, life is revealed.

The Prism of Emotion

Colors dance through the mind's eye,
Shifting shades of joy and sigh.
Rays of happiness touch the skin,
While shadows whisper, deep within.

Every moment, a spectrum bright,
A kaleidoscope caught in light.
Love's tender hue, the gray of pain,
In this prism, we all remain.

Reflections shimmer, bend and twist,
In laughter's glow, in sorrow's mist.
Life's vibrant palette, a fleeting game,
In each color's touch, we find our name.

Through the prism, we see the whole,
The depths of the heart, the spirit's soul.
In every hue, a truth revealed,
In the colors of life, we are healed.

The Mosaic of Dreams

Scattered pieces, bright and worn,
In the fabric of night, our hopes are born.
Each shard a wish, a fragment of light,
In the mosaic we build from dreams at night.

Tales of tomorrow, whispered in sleep,
Shimmering visions, buried deep.
With every heartbeat, each breath we take,
We craft our stories, awake or awake.

Colors collide, ignite the soul,
A dance of shadows, making us whole.
From tiny tiles, a grandeur grows,
In the mosaic of dreams, anything goes.

Piecing together what we believe,
With every heartbeat, we dare to dream.
In the night's embrace, our spirits sing,
In this mosaic, we find our wings.

Textures of My Thoughts

Rough and smooth, the mind's expanse,
Woven threads in a quiet dance.
Beneath the surface, layers unfold,
Tales of the heart, waiting to be told.

Crimson threads of passion's fire,
Gentle wisps of whispered desire.
In every texture, feeling aligns,
In the fabric of thought, love intertwines.

Silken strands of dreams caress,
While jagged edges reveal distress.
The tapestry grows, a vibrant swirl,
In the textures of thoughts, life's colors unfurl.

From whispers soft to thunderous roars,
In every texture, my essence pours.
Crafting a narrative, rich and bold,
In the textures of my thoughts, stories unfold.

Tints of Triumph and Tears

In shadows cast by hopes anew,
We rise from thorns and feel the dew.
Each tear a tale, each laugh a cheer,
In every heart, we find our sphere.

Bright colors blend, the pain and pride,
In whispered dreams, the echoes glide.
Through bitter storms, we learn to sing,
With every fall, our spirits swing.

A tapestry of joy and strife,
Unfolds the beauty in our life.
With triumphs bold, we chart our way,
Each tear a pearl, by night and day.

So let us dance on edges fine,
With courage strong, we boldly shine.
In tints of triumph, tears will flow,
Together, side by side, we grow.

The Harmonies Within

In the quiet corners of my mind,
Soft melodies of love unwind.
Each heartbeat plays a gentle tune,
In tranquil nights and glowing noon.

Whispers of hope weave through the air,
Notes of laughter, free from care.
In every sigh, a story told,
In every dream, a heart of gold.

The pulses of life, a wondrous dance,
Revealing truths, a sweet romance.
With every breath, a symphony,
Unfolds the world's great mystery.

Let the harmonies guide our way,
Through night's embrace and light of day.
Within our souls, a song divine,
Together, forever, hearts align.

Silhouettes in a Falling Light

As dusk descends, the shadows play,
Silhouettes dance in twilight's sway.
With every color fading slow,
The world reveals its hidden glow.

In fleeting moments, dreams take flight,
Wings unfurl in the soft twilight.
Each shape a story, whispered low,
In breaths of wind, the rivers flow.

The beauty found in dusk's embrace,
Shadows draped on earth's soft face.
In gentle hues, our fears take flight,
Silhouettes gleam in the falling light.

Let us cherish these fleeting views,
In silence shared, the heart renews.
For in this twilight, life's made bright,
We find our peace in the fading light.

Unveiling My Inner Landscapes

Into the depths where secrets dwell,
I wander through my hidden shell.
Each corner turned, a tale unfolds,
In shades of warmth, my spirit holds.

Mountains rise, and valleys wide,
Where dreams and fears often collide.
Through forests deep, I carve my way,
In whispers soft, my heart will stay.

I paint my world with brush of thought,
In every stroke, a lesson taught.
With colors bright, my heart explores,
In sacred spaces, joy restores.

So here I stand, my truth in sight,
Unveiling all, I heed the light.
In landscapes vast, both wild and free,
I discover myself, endlessly.

Colors Blended with Time

In twilight's hue, stories unfold,
Shades of the past, in whispers told.
Crimson of laughter, azure of tears,
Mingling in memories, through all the years.

The gold of the dawn, brightening skies,
With each brushstroke, a moment flies.
Emerald dreams beneath the night,
Colors that shimmer, in soft twilight.

Threads of the future, woven with grace,
In every shadow, a lingering trace.
Time spills its pigments, in vibrant streams,
Crafting a tapestry, spun from our dreams.

In the gallery of life, we all reside,
With canvases rich, emotions collide.
As colors blend, so do we find,
The essence of living, in our heart's kind.

The Echoing Canvas of Conscience

On a stark canvas, thoughts take flight,
Each stroke reveals the depths of night.
Echoes of choices, both right and wrong,
Resonate softly, a haunting song.

Colors of guilt, a heavy gray,
Splashes of joy, brightening the day.
In each corner, shadows reside,
Reflecting the battles we try to hide.

A palette of truth, ever so bold,
Painting our stories, both brash and cold.
Every reflection, a chance to change,
Awareness grows, unbound and strange.

In this gallery, we learn and grow,
The echoing tales of our inner flow.
With each creation, we redefine,
The colors of conscience, a dance divine.

Whirlwinds of Internal Palette

In the heart's whirlwind, colors collide,
Swirls of emotion, we cannot hide.
With strokes of passion, we create,
A vibrant chaos that seals our fate.

Reds of anger, blues of despair,
Greens of envy linger in the air.
The whirlwind spins, a tempest's wail,
Echoing loudly, a heart's frail tale.

Yet within the storm, a spark of light,
Yellows of hope break through the night.
Every hue holds a silent power,
Transforming pain into blooms of a flower.

With each swirl, we paint our fears,
Merging colors through the flowing years.
In this internal dance, we find release,
Whirlwinds of palette, a search for peace.

Chasing the Colors Within

I wander through valleys, in search of the hue,
Colors of silence, whispering true.
Chasing the shadows that linger and play,
Hues of the heart, by night and by day.

Each color a story, a dream to unfold,
Patterns of longing, in tales untold.
Violets of visions, the past lingers on,
In the palette of memory, dusk until dawn.

With each brush stroke, I sketch my desires,
Flames of ambition, igniting the fires.
Yellows of laughter, a canvas of glee,
Chasing the colors, to set my heart free.

In the journey of self, I find every shade,
Through trials and triumphs, the colors cascade.
So here's to the chase, a life to explore,
Within every hue, my spirit will soar.